Spotlight on
Kids Can Code

What Is
USER INTERFACE DESIGN?

Patricia Harris

PowerKiDS press

New York

Published in 2018 by The Rosen Publishing Group, Inc.
29 East 21st Street, New York, NY 10010

Copyright © 2018 by The Rosen Publishing Group, Inc.

All rights reserved. No part of this book may be reproduced in any form without permission in writing from the publisher, except by a reviewer.

First Edition

Editor: Melissa Raé Shofner
Book Design: Michael J. Flynn
Interior Layout: Rachel Rising

Photo Credits: Cover shapecharge/Getty Images; pp. 1, 3–24 (coding background) Lukas Rs /Shutterstock.com; pp. 5, 16 Rawpixel.com/Shutterstock.com; p. 6 LINE ICONS/Shutterstock.com; p. 6 La Gorda/Shutterstock.com: p. 7 Denys Prykhodov/Shutterstock.com; p. 8 Castleski/Shutterstock.com; p. 10 PeoGeo/Shutterstock.com; p. 11 Stanisic Vladimir/Shutterstock.com; p. 13 By Have a nice day Photo/Shutterstock.com; p. 14 Kmann/Shutterstock.com;p. 17 Dragon Images/Shutterstock.com; p. 18 ronstik/Shutterstock.com; pp. 19, 21 wavebreakmedia/Shutterstock.com; p. 22 MPFphotography/ Shutterstock.com.

Library of Congress Cataloging-in-Publication Data

Names: Harris, Patricia, 1943 October 17- author.
Title: What is user interface design? / Patricia Harris.
Description: New York : PowerKids Press, [2018] | Series: Spotlight on kids can code | Includes bibliographical references and index.
Identifiers: LCCN 2017000181| ISBN 9781508155287 (pbk. book) | ISBN 9781508154822 (6 pack) | ISBN 9781508155171 (library bound book)
Subjects: LCSH: User interfaces (Computer systems)–Juvenile literature.
Classification: LCC QA76.9.U83 H365 2018 | DDC 005.4/37–dc23
LC record available at https://lccn.loc.gov/2017000181

Manufactured in the United States of America

CPSIA Compliance Information: Batch #BS17PK: For Further Information contact Rosen Publishing, New York, New York at 1-800-237-9932

Contents

What Is UI Design?....................4

Icons from the Past..................6

Input Controls 8

Navigation Controls 10

Icons in Use Today.................12

Rules for Design...................14

The Nuts and Bolts.................18

Getting Started in UI Design.......20

Beyond the Basics..................22

Glossary...........................23

Index..............................24

Websites...........................24

What Is UI Design?

Have you ever opened a new app or program and begun using it without much trouble? Using a new program without any trouble is a sign of quality user interface (UI) design. UI design focuses on the user's interaction with the computer **output** on the screen. Good UI design improves a user's experience by giving the user easy-to-understand design elements on the screen.

User interface designers may work with user experience (UX) designers, and their jobs may sometimes overlap. Both types of designers work on creating easy-to-use **software** and websites. UX designers work on making websites and programs easy to use. UI designers focus on the elements users see as they use software or a website to accomplish what they want to do. UI designers are concerned with how a website or program looks and how users interact with it.

The jobs of UI and UX designers often overlap, but their focus can be very different.

Icons from the Past

User interface designers think about how users perform tasks and the types of activities they will need to complete. They try to design the on-screen elements that users see in a way that makes tasks easier to finish. These elements, called interface elements, include things such as the **font**, color scheme, and various icons.

Many interface icons have been in use for some time, so users are familiar with them and know what to expect from them. The "play" button for most music players today has the same right-facing triangle that appeared on **cassette players** decades ago. The play icon still appears on DVD and CD players. The "record" icon in an app is often a microphone icon or just a red button. Both the microphone and the red button are symbols that come from recording equipment used in the past.

MICROPHONE

RECORD ICON

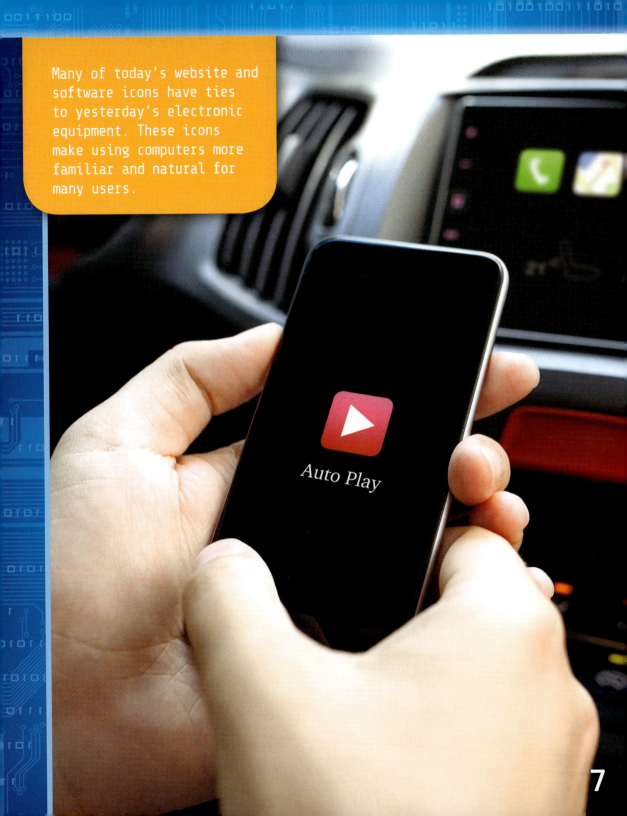

Many of today's website and software icons have ties to yesterday's electronic equipment. These icons make using computers more familiar and natural for many users.

Input Controls

Input controls are interface elements that are meant to get a response from users. These controls can be common things such as text fields, check boxes, and buttons. While UX designers may indicate the type of input control to be used, the design chosen for the control is generally up to the UI designers. There are many options to choose from.

Some web pages have a very simple layout with few input controls. The opening page to Chrome, the Google **web browser**, has a search box, spaces for recently viewed pages, buttons to take users to different Google sites, an icon that launches various Google apps, a notifications button, and an account information button. There's not much on the screen, but users have a world of knowledge at their fingertips.

Input controls such as buttons, toggles, and text fields allow users to interact with websites and software. The more familiar the controls are to users, the easier it is to use the websites and software.

INPUT NAME	EXAMPLES	QUICK FACT
buttons		Buttons can be plain, have images on them, or have text added. They can either look very modern or they can look like buttons from older equipment with which people are familiar.
text fields	FIRST NAME e.g. Bob EMAIL ADDRESS e.g. bob@mail.com **SUBMIT** FIRST NAME _ _ _ _ _ _ _ _ _ _ _ _ _ _	These fields look like the blanks one would fill in on a paper form. Today, UI designers may also choose to use lines instead of boxes.
toggles	ON OFF	Toggles work just like the light switches we flip on and off in our everyday lives

Navigation Controls

Navigation controls make it easy to get from one screen to another when using the Internet or an app or program. If movement between pages is hard, users may become annoyed with the process and not finish their task. On websites where items may be purchased, a shopping cart icon makes it easy to buy things. It just takes a click! The shopping cart is an icon used as a navigation tool. Rather than using text, the trend today is to use icons.

A "breadcrumb" trail is a list of the pages a user has visited on the way to their current website. "Breadcrumbs" were once used as navigation controls, but they don't work with many of today's sites. Designers must find new ways for users to navigate the Internet. For example, many sites, such as Amazon, display pictures of recently viewed items.

Using pictures to show recently viewed items allows online shoppers to navigate back to things they've looked at in the past.

Icons in Use Today

Today, UI designers often use icons to allow users to make choices or access additional information. Icons work great on mobile devices because they're generally easier to tap than words. Icons also save space on a computer screen so more choices can be displayed at once.

Many controls and icons are almost universally recognizable, such as a magnifying glass for "search," envelope for "e-mail," and a gear for "settings." The three-line "hamburger" icon is an old icon that's becoming more recognizable today. When used on websites in the past, it often represented a simple drop-down list of items. Today, it's used to indicate a navigation menu—a drop-down list of clickable links that bring users to related web pages. This change may cause confusion for some users who were familiar with the icon's original use.

E-MAIL ICON

HAMBURGER ICON

Icons used for iPhone apps come together in a set so that UI designers use them **consistently** across all new apps. Android icons are similarly packaged.

Rules for Design

The KISS rule (keep it simple stupid) is one of the most important things to remember in UI design. Keeping things simple means the designer should only include necessary information to avoid possible **distractions**. The design should be kept uncluttered so users know what a web page is about with just a quick glance. It's also important for UI designers to understand that just because they *can* do something doesn't mean they *should*. Ease of use should always come first. When a web page contains too many elements, viewers may get confused and lose interest.

UI designers need to be consistent in their work and pay close attention to details. While most people may not see the tiny things that aren't quite right with a website, small errors will eventually add up. Users will end up thinking the site is poorly designed.

There are many things UI designers need to think about when designing websites and apps.

OTHER RULES FOR UI DESIGNERS

- Be consistent. Use common elements and icons throughout the design.

- Choose font styles for clarity, or clearness. Too much bold is distracting and unusual styles may be difficult to read.

- Keep actions as much like real life as possible. When adding a button to a design, make sure it works like a button.

- Use color carefully. Don't use too many highlights and only use them to indicate important actions. Also, make sure colors work together. Reading blue text on a red background is not easy.

- Word messages clearly and make sure they're correct. Mistakes in text, even simple grammar errors, may distract the user.

UI designers also have rules for the big picture of design. Users should always be told what is happening or what they need to do. If the computer needs time to gather data, the user should be made aware of it. If an error occurs, there should be a **logical** way to correct it.

Designers also need to consider page layout, especially how it will affect first-time users. What's the first information a user will need and the first thing they must do to move on? The layout of the first page should make it easy to find the correct information and take the needed action. A clean layout includes clear actions, easy-to-use control icons, and groups of similar items. Users should have choices available, but not everything has to be shown at once. Some items should be hidden until they're needed.

Users may wonder why nothing is happening when actually the computer is just taking some time to do its job. A message that tells users to wait will help avoid upsetting them.

The Nuts and Bolts

The UI designer's job requires using **psychology**, programming knowledge, and creative design to make an **aesthetic** and effective online user interface. The design process can vary from company to company. It can include collecting information from the customer and the UX designer, sketching, and detailed design work. UI designers determine the layout of the app or web page, the fonts and colors to be used, and how the input and navigation controls will be designed. Then they might pass the information on as a **prototype** to software engineers who will design the actual interface.

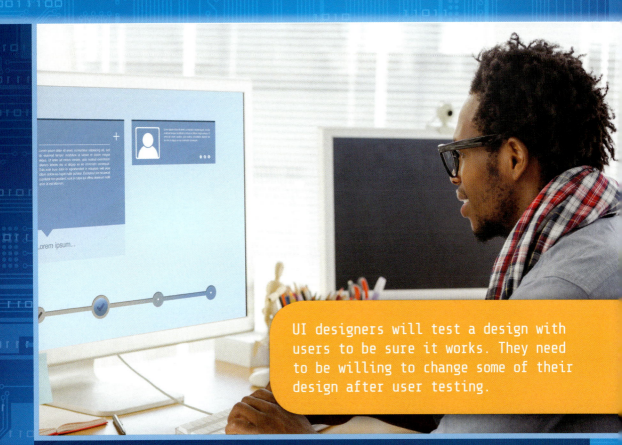

UI designers will test a design with users to be sure it works. They need to be willing to change some of their design after user testing.

Coding for an app is usually done by someone else, but the UI designer may do the coding for websites using programming languages such as HTML, CSS, or JavaScript. Web design may require more interaction with customers than app design. Customers may have ideas for their web pages that really aren't good designs.

19

Getting Started in UI Design

Does user interface design sound like a career you'd be interested in? There are many ways to get started in UI design. One way is to go to college and get a degree in computer science, engineering, or information systems. Taking courses in graphic, or image, design or another artistic field is also a good idea. Some people attend a **technical school** or take part in an online program. Some people teach themselves about UI design.

Whatever educational path you chose, be sure to build a portfolio. A portfolio is a collection of your work that shows off your skills. You should also have a website and social media pages that feature good UI design. You can gain experience and build your portfolio through **internships** or contract jobs. Contract jobs are short-term, project-focused jobs, often at the entry level.

Breaking the Code

UI designers take a variety of courses. Some are related to print and web graphic-design tools such as Adobe Creative Suite programs. UI designers also learn about branding and logo design, type styles, and color theory. Other courses focus on working with databases, frequently used coding languages, and testing methods.

To get a degree in computer science, students must take a variety of courses. Many also take part in an internship.

Beyond the Basics

Becoming a user interface designer requires skills beyond just being able to use the tools of the job. UI designers must care about aesthetics. They must care about the details of an app or website that make it easy to use. They must also care about people. UI design is all about helping people complete their online tasks in an easy, effective, and enjoyable way.

Designers must be able to work as part of a team and have good communication skills. They work with software designers, programmers, and business managers, and they may need to "sell" their design to all these different people. A love of learning is also important because UI design is a changing field. Designers need to keep up with changing design tools and new trends. If you like computers and possess these qualities and skills, UI design may be for you!

Glossary

aesthetic: Pleasing in appearance.

cassette player: A machine that can play back recorded sound on an item called a cassette.

consistency: Agreement or harmony between parts or elements.

distraction: Something that draws attention away from something else.

font: A set of type (letters, numbers, and other characters) that share one style and often one size.

input: Information that is entered into a computer.

internship: A job done—often without pay—in order to gain experience.

logical: In a way that makes sense.

output: The information produced by a computer.

prototype: An original on which a new thing is modeled.

psychology: The study of the mind and behavior.

software: Programs that run on computers and perform certain functions.

technical school: A place that provides specialized training for a specific career, trade, or profession.

web browser: A computer program that allows users to search the Internet.

Index

A
Amazon, 10
Android, 13
apps, 4, 6, 8, 10, 13, 15, 18, 19, 22

B
"breadcrumb" trail, 10
buttons, 6, 8, 9, 15

C
Chrome, 8
coding, 19, 20
color, 6, 15, 18, 20
CSS, 19

F
font, 6, 15, 18

G
Google, 8

H
HTML, 19

I
icons, 6, 7, 8, 10, 12, 13, 15, 16
input controls, 8, 9, 18
interface elements, 6, 8
iPhone, 13

J
JavaScript, 19

K
KISS rule, 14

N
navigation controls, 10, 18

P
portfolio, 20
prototype, 19
psychology, 18

T
text fields, 8, 9
toggles, 9

U
user experience (UX) design, 4, 5, 8, 18

Websites

Due to the changing nature of Internet links, PowerKids Press has developed an online list of websites related to the subject of this book. This site is updated regularly. Please use this link to access the list: www.powerkidslinks.com/skcc/uid